Welcome

Like all Wizoo Quick Starts, this book is designed to help you get a handle on this topic as swiftly and easily as possible. To this end, the Quick Starts are written in concise, easy-to-understand language, and include CD-ROMs that provide you with hands-on experience.

Quick Start "Home Recording" provides an introduction to the working methods used in a home studio by an audio engineer—you, that is. This guide describes the equipment that makes up a studio and explains how to use it. Turning the spotlight on functions and features, it will help you master the sound-sculpting tools so that you can make the most out of your home studio setup.

Here's hoping you enjoy reading, listening, and trying things out. Above all, I wish you lots of success learning the ropes!

Peter Gorges, Publisher

1 BOOK
1 DISC

WIZOO Quick Start

Ingo Raven
Home Recording

Imprint

Author   Ingo Raven
Publisher   Peter Gorges

Cover art   design box, Ravensburg, Germany
Editor   Reinhard Schmitz
Interior design and layout   Uwe Senkler

Copyright © 2001 Wizoo Publishing GmbH, Bremen, Germany
This edition distributed throughout the world by
Music Sales Corporation.

Order No.   WZ 00721
International Standard Book Number   0-8256-1908-4

Exclusive Distributors:
Music Sales Corporation
257 Park Avenue South, New York, NY 10010 USA

Music Sales Limited
8/9 Frith Street, London W1D 3JB England

Music Sales Pty. Limited
120 Rothschild Street, Rosebery, Sydney, NSW 2018, Australia

Printed in the United States of America
by Vicks Lithograph and Printing Corporation

Table of Contents

Table of Contents

The Big Picture

1

Not so long ago professional quality studio devices were all but unaffordable for the average home studio buff. That changed markedly owing to the digital revolution. Sparing the wallet and spoiling the home recordist, digital technology delivers excellent audio quality and affords us many exciting new possibilities.

Unlike traditional tape recording, digital audio generates data which may be edited, processed, stored, and played back on a computer. Today we enjoy access to music software with amazing capabilities—these applications can do everything a conventional studio can do, and lots of wild and wonderful stuff that traditional analog studios will never be able to do. For this reason, digital technology plays a feature role this book.

Multitrack Recording

In contemporary music productions, instruments are generally recorded separately, and, more often than not, sequentially. This is the only way we can address each instrument individually and manipulate the volume and tone of each track when it comes time to mix. To that end, your recording gear should offer plenty of tracks. In the best-case scenario, you will have a track available for every instrument you want to record. Before you start thinking that a handful will do, note that drums consist of many different instruments such as toms and cymbals. You may at some point want to record these separately.

Recording Software

Recording software is the virtual alter ego of a multitrack tape machine. Recording applications are commonly referred to as "sequencers" or "audio/MIDI sequencers."

This type of application provides all the tools you need to do everything from arrange and edit to mix and master tracks. In fact, it shoehorns all the components of a music studio—tape machine, mixer, signal processors—into a PC. This software affords you untold possibilities, eclipsing anything analog or mechanical solutions are able to offer.

MIDI and Audio

One of the issues a fledgling home recordist is confronted with is the distinction between two signal types, MIDI and audio.

In this context, "audio" refers to electrical signals that are converted into sound. In short, this is an audible signal.

When you are working with electronic sound generators, you can also record control messages called *MIDI* data. Rather than capturing the sound of a piano, the recording device records a command that tells a MIDI instrument to play a piano sound.

MIDI has a few advantages over audio:

❖ Information defining notes and other musical data may be processed, edited, corrected, changed, deleted and copied in a computer after it has been recorded.

❖ You can actually swap sounds after you recorded them. A case in point: A signal that you initially recorded as a piano can be played back with an organ sound. And you can layer sounds on top of the original sound.

❖ MIDI information amounts to just a tiny fraction of the data generated by audio signals, and a song comprised of audio data is several thousand times the size of a comparable MIDI song. MIDI data hardly burdens the computer.

Logic Audio by Emagic and Cubase VST by Steinberg are good examples of tried-and-true recording programs, applications that have proven their mettle in countless real-world situations. Both offer all the functions of a studio, and both are able to record MIDI as well as audio tracks.

MIDI is a communication standard for digital musical instruments and computers.

You'll find a demo version of Cubase VST in the data section of the enclosed CD.

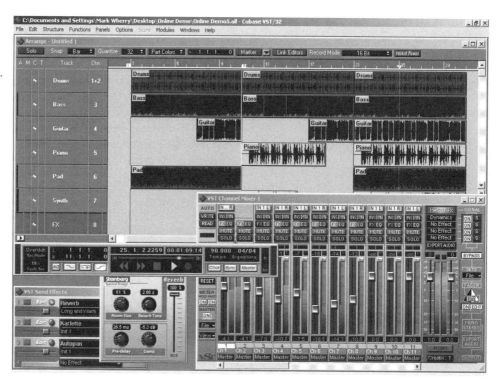

Multitrack Recorders

Eschewing the PC revolution, many home recordists prefer to work with self-contained multitrack recorders. Let's take a look at the most common types.

Cassette Multitrackers

These are cassette tape machines that can record several tracks—normally, four or eight—onto an analog audio cassette. Frequently they are equipped with very basic mixers. Once the home recordist's bread-and-butter device, it has largely been supplanted by digital alternatives offering better recording quality.

The Tascam 424 MkIII is a cassette multitracker featuring four tracks.

MD Multitrackers

MD multitrackers record audio in digital format to tracks on a *MiniDisc* (MD). Though owing to data reduction, an MD multitracker's sound quality can't compete with that of a CD, it is still better than anything analog cassette recorders are capable of delivering. Most MD multitrackers ship with built-in mixers.

MiniDisc: A digital storage medium for audio data developed by Sony for the hi-fi market.

HD Multitrackers

HD multitrackers record audio in digital format to tracks on a hard disk (HD). A mixer is often on board, and some devices even offer one or several effects.

HD multitrackers let you record loss-free—you can even copy entire musical passages from track to track. This spells convenience galore, and it saves oodles of time. For example, you could record a challenging harmony part, and once your vocalists get it right, copy it to all choruses of your song rather than recording additional performances.

How small can a studio be? As small as the Roland VS-890 featuring a mixer, effects and CD burner support.

One of the tremendous advantages that an HD multitracker has over its mechanical predecessors is the so-called "virtual track." It lets you record and play back an amazing number of audio tracks. A minor downside is that you have to track sequentially. The number of tracks that you can record and play back simultaneously is determined by the number of physical inputs/outputs you have available.

Many HD multitrackers come with a mixer, an effects processor, and a port for connecting a CD burner. That makes this type of HD recorder a real hardware alternative for recordists who want to steer clear of a computer.

The Computer as a Multitracker

Of all the home studio alternatives, the computer no doubt offers the most options. A *soundcard* or audio card must be installed to get audio signals into the computer and back out again. In addition, you will require some type of recording software.

The advantages of a computer-based recording setup are many:

❖ You can work comfortably and conveniently on a monitor and need not struggle with tiny displays.

❖ All EQ and effect settings may be stored with the composition. This makes it so much easier to administer songs.

❖ You can select hardware and software freely, and extend your recording setup or swap components later down the road. As your skills and confidence improve, your ambitions are likely to grow. You can make your computer system "grow" with them.

❖ A computer-based setup requires far less space than outboard gear.

❖ State-of-the-art computers deliver performance aplenty, which translates into lots of audio and MIDI tracks, virtual mixers, effects, and even instruments. That, in turn, translates into more fun.

❖ Software effects and instruments take up no space, and you get several versions of the same device/instrument for the price of one.

There is of course a downside:

Soundcard: A plug-in card that equips a computer with audio ports and, in many cases, a sound generator.

❖ The number and variety of available hardware and software boggles the mind, the configuration possibilities are untold. It is scarcely possible that all components will harmonize. Specialized devices are more stable than everything-but-the-kitchen-sink systems. Computers are prone to "crash."

❖ Hardware systems are more portable and far more suitable for the stage than unwieldy computers.

❖ Many recordists get a bigger kick from twiddling real knobs than handling virtual on-screen controls via mouse.

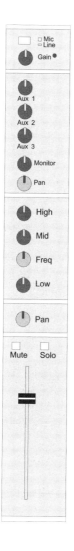

The Mixer

The mixing console is the hub of every studio. All microphones, instruments, recording devices, and signal processors, as well as the monitoring system are connected to it.

As you can well imagine, it takes loads of switches, buttons and knobs to direct the signal flow between these devices and control the volume and shape the sound of all instruments.

Generally ranging from 4 to 64, the number of channels determines the size and price of the mixer.

A typical channel strip looks something like this:

At the top of the strip there is ordinarily a switch or button for selecting the type of input (line, instrument, tape, mic) and a "gain" knob that dials in a suitable level of preamplification for the input signal.

Located below these control features are knobs for addressing effect devices via so-called "aux" busses and the monitor circuit. The latter lets musicians hear their instruments and other signals routed through the mixer during a recording session.

The voicing section (several tone controls that are collectively called an equalizer or "EQ") consists of knobs that amplify (boost) or attenuate (cut) different frequency ranges. More on the subject of EQs in the section "Making the Most of Equalizers" on page 30.

The panorama knob ("pan") determines the position of the signal in the stereo spread.

At the bottom are sliding volume controls called "faders" and the "mute" and "solo" buttons. Mute lets you silence the channel, the solo button silences all others so that only this channel remains audible.

Effect Devices

The following types of effect devices (also called signal processors and effectors) are commonly found in studios.

Multi-Effect Devices

One multi-effect device with lots of effects on board is cheaper than a crowd of stand-alone devices, each specializing in one or two effects. A multi-effector is also more convenient for creating complex combinations using several effects simultaneously. On the downside, the quality of each effect can rarely match that of a special-purpose tool. This is especially true of effects like reverb and delay, which are known for their healthy appetite for computing performance.

The Virtualizer DSP 1000, a multi-effector by Behringer.

Specialized Effect Devices

Ideally, the audio professional wants to own a device for every effect. Alas you need deep pockets to satisfy that gear lust. In the bang-for-buck sweepstakes, stand-alone solutions will always finish last behind multi-effect devices. If you want to go the same route, you must buy, find a place for, and connect one device for every effect. Bear in mind that fine-tuning sophisticated signal processors takes a lot longer than simply loading a preset hall/chorus/delay combination.

Software Effects

Plug-in: A miniature program that plugs into (hence the name) a larger host application, which then controls it.

The advantages of a computer-based setup extends to effects: Most recording programs ship with onboard effects, which means you don't need to beg, steal, or borrow hardware to make funny noises. In addition, almost every recording software lets you add further effects called *plug-ins*, many of which are available for free (hence the term freeware).

Cubase VST comes with piles of effect plug-ins, among them this phaser.

While you must buy two reverb devices if you want to use two different reverb effects at the same time, you can activate as many virtual versions of most plug-ins as your PC's CPU can compute. Be aware, though, that some plug-ins are notorious chow hounds when it comes to computing resources, so less is often more.

The Monitoring System

Special loudspeakers called monitors are used to audition tracks during production. Unlike hi-fi speakers, monitors are not designed to deliver the most stirring audio experience the given price tag will buy. Their purpose is to convert electrical signals into sound waves as faithfully as possible (that's what neutral response is all about). "Active" monitors have built-in amps designed specifically for the given speakers, while "passive" monitors require external amps.

Your home stereo will do in a bind. On the downside, it probably won't deliver neutral response (uncolored sound reinforcement). On the upside, you are accustomed to its sound so you'll find it easier to pinpoint problems in the mix.

Master Recording Devices

Once a song has been mixed down to a stereo signal, it must be re-recorded to a medium such as DAT or CD. If you own a computer equipped with a CD burner, you can spare yourself the expense of a master recording device by converting your song directly into a file and burning it onto CD.

Microphones

You will need microphones if you want to record acoustic signals like vocals or a guitar. The next chapter offers tips on selecting suitable microphones and deploying them for different recording situations.

Tips on Recording

2

Before I introduce you to the techniques for recording various instruments, I would like to share a few words of wisdom on auditioning tracks, a process that audio engineers call "monitoring."

How to Monitor Tracks

Musicians must be able to hear themselves and other musicians as well as previously recorded instruments while they are laying down tracks, and they must be able to hear these signals in a balance and volume that they feel comfortable with.

When you are recording acoustic signals, the musician must employ headphones for monitoring purposes, otherwise the sound of the monitor speakers will "spill" over into the microphones.

Almost all mixers are equipped with monitor bus knobs that let you route each channel's signal into the monitor mix. If necessary, you could also misappropriate an effect send knob and the "aux" bus for this purpose. To this end, all you have to do is connect the effect send output to the monitoring amp.

When you record with a computer, a little monster called *latency* may rear its ugly head. This means that the signal you are recording is sent out over the soundcard's output with an audible delay. The musician hears it a split-sec-

Latency: Delay caused by the time it takes the computer to calculate and output audio data.

ond later, which makes it impossible to keep good time or, as studio wizards call it, play in the pocket.

> If the problem can't be fixed by adjusting settings on the computer, you can solve it by connecting a small mixer in front of the computer and using it for the monitor mix.

In the following sections, I'll give you a few tips on recording different sound sources. Note that these refer to the CD's audio examples.

Vocals

◎ CD Track 2
Vocal tracks recorded with a microphone placed at a distance of 20cm, 50cm and 1m.

A distance of some 10 to 50cm from the vocalist's mouth to the microphone is standard when recording vocals using high-quality studio microphones. The sound of the room becomes more prominent as the distance increases.

Pop Filters

When articulating consonants like "p" or "t," the human voice makes a speech sound that stops and then releases an air stream. Sensitive microphones pick that popping sound up so that it can become audible in your mix. The device used to interdict this noise is called "pop filter."

◎ CD Track 3
Phrase first without and then with a pop filter.

A pop filter consists of a rim with some type of mesh material covering that interrupts the air stream. It is attached to the microphone stand or a separate stand. In either case, it is placed between the microphone's diaphragm and the vocalist's mouth.

Acoustic Guitar

If you want to capture the sound of an acoustic guitar as faithfully as possible, you should always use the highest quality microphone you are willing and able to afford. A pickup won't do.

By placing the microphone in various positions, you have a decisive hand in determining the tone of the instrument. Bottom end is most prominent near the sound hole, the top end increases as you move closer to the bridge. The sound is warmest with the mic pointed towards the neck, but you will also capture a lot of fretting noises.

⊚ CD Track 4
Guitar with a microphone placed 30cm away from and facing the sound hole, then the same distance facing the bridge, and finally facing the middle of the fret board.

Don't point the mic directly toward the sound hole when you're recording strummed guitars because you'll get a "boomy" bottom end. Good results can also be achieved by placing one mic over the bridge and another over the neck but pointing towards the body.

Electric Guitar

You have two options for recording electric guitars—miking up the amp or using one of the recording preamps on the market.

Recording without Microphones

Your easiest option is to plug the guitar directly into a mixer channel. Convenient as this option, we're not talking sonic fireworks here. That direct sound is often lackluster or just plain lacking.

21

◎ CD Track 5
A phrase recorded via direct out, then with a mic on the speaker.

Many guitar amps feature a special output called a "direct out." As its name would suggest, it connects directly to a mixer. The muddy tone that you get when you plug right into a mixer channel won't be a problem. This sound is extremely bright, certainly more so than what you are accustomed to hearing from an amp. The reason for this is that the amp's speaker normally dampens the higher frequencies.

◎ CD Track 6
Guitar recorded via a tube preamp (Hughes & Kettner Tubeman), then a POD.

Of late, countless devices simulating the sounds of legendary guitar amps have flooded the market. Witness the Line 6 POD, perhaps the most fashionable of these amp emulators. The sound is convincing, handling is a breeze. My tip: Don't knock it 'till you've tried it. I like it and chances are you will too!

The POD by Line 6

Recording Electric Guitars with Microphones

Even if the benefits of direct recording are persuasive (your neighbors will continue to treat you civilly, sounds are easily reproduced), there's just something about a righteous tube amp cranked to the verge of breaking up that makes the musician's heart beat faster. The classic method of capturing that vibe is to "close" mic the amp— i.e. stick a microphone right in its face.

The position of the mic relative to the speaker is important as this has a formative influence on tone. A speaker projects high frequencies out from the center in a relatively tight pattern—picture a mildly tapering cone, if you will. The projection pattern of bass frequencies, on the other hand, is not nearly as focused. It radiates fairly evenly in all directions.

In order to capture more of a room vibe, many audio engineers place an additional microphone at a greater distance to the amp (one to several meters). The signal of the microphone placed in front of the speaker is usually the more prominent in the mix.

◎ CD Track 7
A microphone sweeping from one side of the speaker to the other. The high frequencies are strongest near the center position.

◎ CD Track 8
First one microphone placed directly in front of the amp, then another at a distance of about 2m, finally the two together.

Drums

Miking a drum kit is quite a challenge, and there's the problem of opportunity. Not everyone has a studio large enough to accommodate a drummer, nor for that matter an accommodating drummer. Fortunately there are options to having a sweaty stranger thumping skins in the lounge—samplers and drum computers that deliver authentic-sounding drum noises. If recording software yanks your chain, then a software drum computer could be just what the doctor ordered.

VST Drum Sessions

The Steinberg "VST Drum Sessions" for Cubase VST series is a convenient option for endowing your songs with realistic-sounding drum parts. These CDs feature drums grooves recorded live onto up to twelve audio

◎ CD Track 9
An excerpt from the VST Drum Sessions "Rock & Pop."

23

tracks. You can arrange and mix tracks and vary their tempo freely in Cubase.

Drum Computer or Sampler

Sample: In this context, a digital sound bite composed of a single note, tone, or drum hit.

A drum computer is equipped with a nonvolatile memory in which *samples* of the drums and cymbals are stored permanently. You can enter rhythms manually into the device hit by hit, so to speak, and play them back as you please, or you can program grooves on a sequencer program and sync up the drum computer to your song via MIDI.

Though a sampler will put a bigger dent in your wallet than a drum computer, it is the more flexible option. Drum kits featured on sample CD-ROMs may be loaded into a sampler and then played via MIDI. Samplers are also available in virtual form as software instruments.

Drum Loops

A drum loop is simply a pattern with a length of one or several bars that can be played by a sequencer as an endless loop. What's hip about drum loops is that the cream of the crop is recorded by first-rate drummers in top-flight studios—these patterns groove and sound real good. On the downside, drum loops are not known for their overwhelming versatility. You can't adapt them to suit the musical requirements of a song. If you want to insert a wicked breakdown here, a syncopated accent there, or drop two beats elsewhere, be prepared for anything from lots of hassle to total frustration.

To vary the tempo of a drum loop without changing its pitch, you need a feature called *time stretching*. Audio editing software like Steinberg's "Wavelab" offers this feature. Conveniently, a demo version of Wavelab is in the data section of the CD.

There may well be some coloration when you alter the tempo with time stretching—the greater the change, the more audible it becomes.

Recording Drums with Microphones

Usually the best results are achieved when each drum is miked individually. If that's out of the question, record as many instruments as possible separately.

Mic the kick drum from the inside with the mic placed some 10 to 12cm from the rim.

The mic for the snare should point down towards the snare from above. Set it a few centimeters from the rim, roughly pointing to the center of the skin. The snare mic should face away from the hi-hat.

If you are miking open-bottomed toms, you can place the microphones inside them so that they point toward the head. Be aware that this may also capture boomy resonant frequencies. Very uncool, at least for most conventional styles of music. One alternative is to place the microphone outside and a short distance above the tom, orienting it towards the edge of the head.

Use a condenser microphone with a small diaphragm for miking hi-hats, and position it diagonally so that it points to the edge of the hi-hat from above.

Time stretching is the process of lengthening or shortening an audio passage without changing its pitch.

◎ CD Track 10
First the original drum loop, then with tempo change via "time stretching."

Toms produce neither monstrous bottom end nor sizzling top end, so you can get away with using cheaper "leftover" microphones.

25

Overhead: Any mic pointing at a sound source from above.

Cymbals are generally miked with just two *overheads.* Condenser microphones with small diaphragms are your first choice here. Place them to the left and right at a good height over the drum set, or in a "V" formation at the center. They should be set to an angle of some 90 degrees with the right mic trained towards the left half of the drum set, and vice versa.

Other Instruments

Here are a couple of tips on other instruments:

❖ The same principle for guitars recorded direct-to-desk apply to the electric bass.

❖ Record plucked, bowed, and strummed stringed in-struments like mandolins, banjos, fiddles, and so forth using microphones and the same techniques as for acoustic guitars.

❖ Upright and grand pianos are generally recorded with two high-quality microphones. This is rarely an option in the home studio—most of us lack a grand piano, not to mention the floor space to park it in—but you can always fall back to digital pianos or samples.

❖ Woodwind and brass instruments are recorded with a microphone in front of the bell. For saxophone, you can also orient the mic more towards the keys.

Mixing and Effects 3

When it comes time to mix your song, you'll blend the signals of the individual tracks to create a cohesive overall sound. This a creative process much like playing an instrument, and its importance in shaping the final product—your song—should not to be underestimated. You will equalize tracks to sound the way you want them to in the context of the song, dial in the desired balance of levels, and process signals with effects.

Using your mixing console and connected effect devices, your job is to find out what suits each track best in terms of volume, tone, position in the stereo panorama, and effects.

The Dos and Don'ts of Mixing

To master the art of mixing, you must come to understand how one track can influence the sound of another, even how individual frequencies bands of single signal can influence each other. For example, if you boost a certain frequency range of an instrument it will cut through the mix better. That makes it sound louder, so you have to back off its level.

If you turn up the level of one instrument and its frequencies overlap those of another instrument, the former may mask the latter's sound. That second instru-

In the data section of the CD in the "Multitrack" folder, you'll find a Cubase arrangement offering several audio tracks for your experimenting pleasure. To learn more, read the "readme.txt" file.

27

ment suddenly sounds softer and thinner. So you turn up that track, which in turn drowns out others. That brings us to Mix Lesson No. 1: Always keep your ear on the big sonic picture. Don't get into the habit of mixing tracks one after the other in isolation and leaving it at that. Every time you tweak a track, audition it in the context of the overall mix.

Selecting Suitable Levels for Instruments

Choosing the right volume for the individual instruments in the mix boils down to your hearing and taste. Personal preferences aside, there are several avoidable pitfalls for home recordists:

❖ Personal bias. Musicians tend to feature their own instrument very prominently in the mix, often more so than is good for the song.

❖ The "crank-it-dude" syndrome. If an instrument fails to cut through, you don't necessarily have to turn that track up. You may achieve better results by turning down other instruments that share the same frequency range.

❖ Dynamic overkill. The peaks and valleys of signals—instruments that are too soft in some places and too loud in others—should be leveled out using a compressor. For more on this, check out the section "Using Effects" on page 34.

❖ Give it a fair hearing. Audition your mix on as many different systems you can find, as often as you can stomach it. You want the track to sound at least passable everywhere people will hear it.

❖ Don't be afraid to emulate your heroes. Make a habit of comparing your mix with reference CDs of a similar style. Discovering that Jimi Hendrix' axe is considerably softer than your guitar or the kick drum of the latest summer hit is half as massive as the one in your song should give you some food for thought.

EQ'ing

The tone of the various instruments—the relative balance of ranges such as bass, middle and treble frequencies—is shaped using the tone controls of your mixer. Collectively these are called an "equalizer," or "EQ" for short.

On simple equalizers, the individual filters (also called "bands") are set to a fixed frequency. Hi-fi systems offering just one bass and one treble knob are a good example of this breed of EQ. You can vary the amount of cut or boost, but not the frequency. On a three-band EQ, you also get a middle knob.

The amount of amplification (boost) and attenuation (cut) is indicated in decibels (dB). Doubling or halving the signal level is equivalent to a change of some 6dB.

A parametric equalizer lets you determine the frequency as well as the bandwidth (*Q-factor*, Q, or quality) of individual bands. This breed of equalizer is very versatile because it lets you target a specific frequency range, and tune the breadth and depth of the EQ's action to suit the situation.

The *Q-factor* determines the bandwidth of the EQ'd frequency range.

The following figures depict the effect of an equalizer on frequency response. The horizontal axis represents the entire range of audible frequencies (20 to 20,000Hz), the vertical axis indicates level in dB.

29

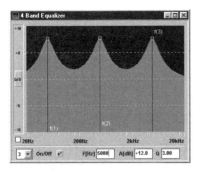

Three filters with frequencies of 50Hz, 500Hz and 5,000Hz. At a Q value of 3.0, each frequency is boosted by +12dB.

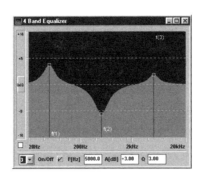

The frequency on the left was boosted by +6dB, in the center it was cut by some −9dB, on the right boosted by +3dB.

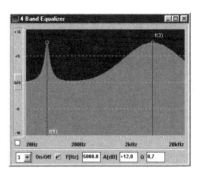

Shown on the left is a narrow-band boost (Q = 10), on the right a broadband boost (Q = 0.7).

◎ CD Track 11
Drum beat, first the original then with different equalizer settings.

Higher quality mixers are generally equipped with a parametric equalizer featuring three or four bands. Less costly consoles often offer hybrid EQs with two parametric filters for the midrange and fixed-frequency bass and treble knobs.

Making the Most of Equalizers

Use equalizers sparingly. In fact, you should only use an EQ to eliminate real problems with a signal's tone. Prefab sounds—samples, drum computer patterns, synthesizer sounds—often sound great right out of the box, and need no EQ'ing. The following table gives you an idea of where the different frequency ranges lie so that you can pinpoint problem areas:

Frequency	Designation	Effect
40—about 120Hz	Bass	Bottom end
About 120—about 1kHz	Lower mids	Fullness
1—5kHz	Upper mids	Transparency
5—20kHz	Treble	Brightness

Perhaps the most common misconceptions is that more is better. Many home recordists will invariably boost a frequency they want to hear more of rather than cutting the frequencies that are masking it. Bear in mind that you can emphasize bottom and top end frequencies by cutting the midrange and slightly boosting the overall level.

On first impression, boosting bass and treble frequencies always sounds better than cutting middle frequencies. However this is due to increased level rather than improved tone. Our ears typically perceive a signal to be fatter, bigger, and better sounding when its level increases.

Leave some room for the characteristic frequencies of individual instruments by backing off these frequencies on the other instruments. This prevents signals from overlapping and muddying the overall sound.

If too many instruments share similar frequencies and occupy the same sonic space so that the mix sounds cluttered, try rethinking your arrangement. Sometimes all it takes to clean up the mess is to transpose one instrument so that its part played an octave higher or lower. This simple remedy will often work wonders, and it's certainly more satisfying than twiddling EQs for hours on end.

Tips on EQ'ing Individual Instruments

Drums

For the obvious reasons, the sound of a kick drum has a lot of bottom end to it. However, the signal also contains a considerable share of higher frequencies ranging up to about 5kHz. Feel free to cut frequencies lower than 40Hz with abandon. It takes a really good monitoring system to even hear them and they usually do more harm than good anyway.

For a fatter sound, boost frequencies in the range of 60 to 100Hz. If the kick drum sounds "mushy," cutting the middle frequencies can cure that ill. Boosting the signal at around 1kHz emphasizes the sound of the mallet hitting the head, boosting it in the 2 to 3kHz range adds presence.

When you want to fatten up the sound of a snare, dial in a broadband bottom end boost by selecting a low Q value. To imitate those huge-sounding snares that were all the rage back in the 70s and 80s, dial in a narrow-band for the fundamental sound of the snare by selecting a high Q value. Boosting the upper mids makes the snare sound harder and tauter. Adjust the top end as you see fit.

For toms, you may cut the upper treble and lower bass frequencies—they rarely deliver any useful frequencies in these ranges. Boost the upper mids for added snap, but make sure that you don't thin out the sound so that it becomes tinny. You can eliminate "boomy" frequencies by cutting the lower mids.

Cymbals and hi-hats usually don't call for much EQ'ing. If you care to bonsai bottom end frequencies, go for it—

top end is all it takes to get a good sound from these instruments. Boosting the treble frequencies will add a nice shimmer to the cymbals. Remember, though, that a little goes long way. If you go overboard, the appeal of all that high-end gloss will soon fade.

Bass

If the bottom end sounds muddy or tubby, try cutting the mids. An extra helping of treble makes slapped bass lines really stand out in the mix.

Guitars

Add lustre and punch to dull guitar sounds by boosting frequencies in the 2 to 5kHz range. If a distorted guitar sounds too scratchy, cut the highest frequencies.

Guitars recorded direct to desk sound better when you boost frequencies in the 3 to 5kHz range and cut all frequencies above 6kHz hard.

Rhythm guitars tend to sit better in the mix if you go easy on the bass. If a track is too dense to cut through cleanly, try dialing in a broadband cut centered around 100Hz.

Keyboards

When tracking keyboards and synthesizers, your best bet is to dial in the sound you want right on the instrument. Then when it comes time to mix, all you have to do is cut any frequencies that mask other parts.

Vocals

The rule for EQ'ing vocals is simple—less is more. Avoid tweaking narrow bandwidths, because it won't take much of this to make a voice sound unnatural. If you do decide to EQ a vocal track, limit your invasive sonic surgery to cutting or boosting broad high and low frequency bands, leaving the mids well enough alone.

Using Effects

Effects can enrich the sound of instruments or voices, make them sit better in the mix, sound more natural, or bend and distort them to points beyond recognition.

Insert Effects and Aux Effects

If you want to process a track with an effect, in most cases you will connect a signal processor to the mixer. There's more than one way to skin that cat, two to be precise.

When you plug a signal processor into an insert, the signal path of that channel is interrupted and the effect is inserted at the same point, hence the name. Any inserted effects device will only affect the channel that it is plugged into. Inserts are used to process the direct signal, which goes out 100% dry and comes back 100% wet (that's audio jargon for "processed"). Equalizers, compressors and distortion modules are typical insert effects.

Aux is short for "auxiliary." The alternative is to connect the signal processor to the mixing desk's effects or *aux* bus. This circuit taps into a channel bus, routing its signal to an effect device. Rather than being a roadblock that stops the signal flow and detours it to the processor, an aux bus is like a Y-junction that parts the signal flow. The direct or dry signal remains unaffected; the signal processor generates an effects or a wet signal that you can blend with the original dry signal to taste. Note that a signal processor may be addressed by several channels. Since every channel has its own "send" circuit, you can do things like slap more reverb on a snare than on a hi-hat despite the fact that both signals are sent to the same reverb device. Chorus, delay, and reverb are typical aux effects.

The aux bus signal is routed to an effector via the aux send output of the mixing console. The signal is patched back into the mixing console from the signal processor's output to the aux return input. The aux return knob determines the amount of wet signal in the overall mix.

The following diagram depicts both variants schematically.

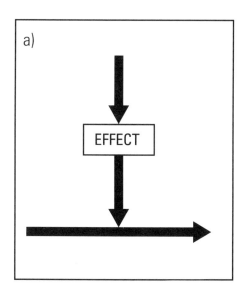
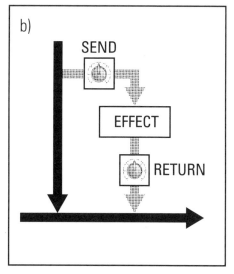

a) The processor is plugged into an insert.
b) The processor is patched into an aux bus.

A few practical tips on effects routing:

❖ By its very nature, an equalizer is an insert processor. If you connect it to an aux bus you won't be able to cut any frequencies!

❖ A compressor processes the original signal to iron out differences in level, so it's definitely an insert processor.

❖ Reverb and delay can go either way. Insert the effector if you want to treat just one channel. If you want to provide several channels with reverb or delay, plug it into the aux bus.

Key Effect Types

Reverb

◎ CD Track 12
Vocal track with reverb

Reverb envelopes a signal with artificial room ambience. It is made up of many reverberations with different delay times. These reflections follow in such close succession that we can no longer distinguish them separately. The effect sounds like a signal bouncing off the walls of a room, fooling our mind into thinking that is what it we are hearing.

A Cubase VST reverb plug-in.

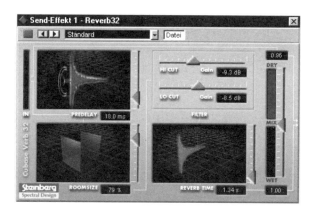

The reverb effect's duration is determined by a parameter called "decay" or "reverb time." The dimensions of the simulated room also influence reverb time; these are defined by the "room size" parameter. You can attenuate high frequencies using the "high damp" or "hi cut" parameter. It lets you simulate rooms with hard, smooth walls (less high end damping) or rooms with sonically assimilative surfaces like upholstered furniture or carpets (lots of high end damping). The "pre-delay" parameter lets you do just that to the reverb effect, delay it for a moment before it kicks in. This gives listeners the impression that they are standing closer to the sound source because they first hear the original and then, a brief but perceptible split second later, the reflections bouncing off the walls.

Most of us prefer to hear bass that is taut and focused. Reverb tends to smear bottom end frequencies all over the place, so exercise restraint when laying reverb on bass and kick drum tracks.

To enhance the transparency and spatial depth of your mix, you can dial different effect send knob settings to lay different types of reverb over the various tracks. Experience teaches us that a little dab will do for rhythm instruments—they tend to sound better with less reverb, while solo instruments and vocals can take a dab more.

Massive reverb creates a majestic sound, so the temptation to pile it on is great. Resist that urge and use reverb discreetly.

> In the folder "Multitrack" on the CD, you'll find an arrangement that you can load to the Cubase demo version. It features a reverb effect. For more on this, check out "readme.txt" in the same folder.

Delay
A delay generates time-based effects like echoes. The most important parameter on this signal processor is "delay time." This is the amount of time that elapses between the original signal and its echo. Sometimes you will want the signal to repeat more than once. You can

determine the number of repetitions using the "feed-back" knob.

These repetitions may occur in time with the music, for example, at eighth or quarter note intervals. The delay time required to do this depends on the tempo of the song. To get these echoes to repeat right on the money, dial in the delay time by trial and error or calculate it.

> In the data section of the CD, you'll find "WizCalc." This handy utility figures out the desired delay time for you.

◎ CD Track 13
Vibraphone with delay, first by an eighth note, then by three eighth notes.

However, you can achieve very interesting effects if the repetitions aren't locked in sync with the beat of the song, or they come at "odd" times, say at intervals of three eighth notes. You'll get a kick out of experimenting with different delay times.

◎ CD Track 14
This guitar was doubled with a short delay.

A delay can also make instruments or vocals sound bigger by duplicating the original signal. In the audio vernacular, this effect is called "doubling." The signal is delayed ever so slightly (some 5 to 40ms) without feedback. To impress friends and family, pan the original and delayed signal hard to the right and left of the stereo image.

> The Cubase arrangement on the CD features a lead guitar line with delay. This delay is plugged in as an insert effect.

Chorus, Phaser, and Flanger

◎ CD Track 15
Guitar phrase with chorus, then phaser and finally flanger.

These three effects are used to introduce some type of movement into a signal, to animate it, or to lend it an artificial, often spacey, flavor.

On most virtual and physical devices you can control the intensity of the effect ("depth," "intensity," "width") and the rate of pitch change ("rate," "frequency," "speed"). These knobs usually let you dial in anything from an extremely slow jet-like effect to a powerful, fast vibrato.

Much like the aforementioned doubling effect, a chorus fattens up signals. A chorus effect splits the signal into various frequency bands, varies their phases and amplitudes, and recombines them. That's a real complicated way of saying that it makes as if more than one instrument is playing the same line.

A flanger routes the wet signal back into the input (there's that "feedback" again). This creates a whooshing sound reminiscent of a starting jet aircraft, which is why back in the dark ages of recording a flanger was also called a "jet effect."

As its name would suggest, a phaser generates a phase modulation that, at its most extreme, sounds similar to the speech of an extremely inebriated person—one big vowel movement, that is. It sounds especially spacey with synthesizer sounds. Careful though, phasers can become an obsession (witness the sad case of Jean-Michel Jarre).

You can try these three effects out using the Cubase arrangement "Multi-track mixed.all" on the CD.

Compressor

Say you recorded a vocal track. It sounds great and sits well in the mix. Yet when you are finished tracking and go to mix the full-blown song you notice that the vocal track is too loud at one spot and too soft at another. What do you? You call on the services of a compressor.

Put simply, a compressor reduces a signal's dynamic range, that is to say the difference in volume between

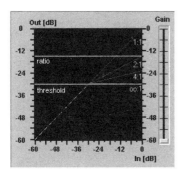

A look at a compressor's "characteristic curve" should make it clearer to you what the "threshold" and "ratio" parameters do. The higher the ratio value, the harder the volume level is cut when it crosses the threshold. That's what causes that sharp bend in the characteristic curve.

soft and loud passages. To do this, it lowers the level of any part of the signal that lies above a variable "threshold" according to a variable "ratio." Using the "attack" parameter, you can also determine if the compressor slam-dunks the volume level immediately after it crosses the threshold or if it gradually backs it off over a certain amount of time. The same thing holds true for the "release" parameter. This is the time it takes for the compressor to release the signal after it has dropped below the threshold.

You may have heard or read that a compressor makes a signal sound "punchier." "How's that," you may ask, "doesn't a compressor lower the volume?" Right, but once those signal peaks are flattened out, you can boost the level of the signal overall. This means that the "average level" of the processed signal is higher than it was before it was processed. The "gain" knob is used to boost the processed signal.

> You can hear a compressor do its thing on a lead guitar in the Cubase arrangement "Multitrack mixed.all" on the CD.

Most compressors offer some kind of visual indicator that makes it easier for you to dial in desirable settings. These displays will in some form indicate when the device is processing the signal too heavily. You don't want to squeeze the life out of every track. Depending on the effect you're after, you should set the "ratio" and "threshold" knobs just high enough to cut off the peaks or tame wildly dynamic tracks. Unless you want to create freaky effects, go easy on the compression.

Mastering—the Final Sonic Buff

4

After you have mixed a song to your satisfaction, it still requires some minor tweaking before you can dump it to CD, DAT, MD, or cassette. This aftertreatment is called "mastering."

In a home studio, mastering should be done on a computer where you can burn the result right onto CD or post it on the Internet. Today there are some great mastering programs available for the home recordist, among them Steinberg's Wavelab and Sonic Foundry's Soundforge.

You'll find a demo version of Wavelab in the data section of the enclosed CD.

Fixing It in the Master Mix

Common to virtually all beginning recordists is a tendency to overemphasize the bottom and top ends while mixing—hey, why not make *everything* sound a little better? The truth is, overkill wears thin after while. Particularly on repeated listening, excessive tweaking is the aural equivalent of running your fingertips down a cheese grater.

Then there is the problem of sonic diversity. Generally you want to release different songs together in a cohesive package, so they shouldn't sound as if they were recorded on different planets.

Conservative EQ'ing can help in both instances. It's a good idea to use CDs as references. Put on a favorite track that sounds like what you're after and attempt to approximate its frequency spectrum.

Ironing Out Levels

As soon as the volume exceeds a value of 0dB, you will hear unpleasant distortion.

Mastering software identifies the highest level (the loudest part of your song) and then boosts the overall volume so that the loudest part has a maximum allowable level of 0dB. This process is called "normalizing."

If you compare your normalized song to a professional production, you will probably find that the latter sounds much louder. How's that, isn't your 0dB equal to their 0dB? Indeed it is. Be aware, though, that normalizing simply references the highest level in the song; it has no influence on the "average level." With all other conditions being equal, the average level determines how loud we perceive a song to be.

Peak: The highest amplitude in an audio section, for instance, in a marked region or an entire song.

When you view an audio signal in a mastering software window, you'll see many *peaks* that rise above the average level. These are surges in level caused by drum hits or other percussive signals. If you decide to crank the level, these peaks will exceed the maximum allowable value of 0dB and generate distortion despite that fact that the levels of the rest of the signal remain well under the 0dB mark.

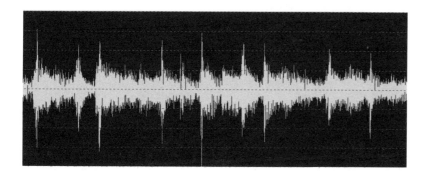

The peak in the center of the picture rules out any further boost in volume.

Since peaks normally come and go very quickly, you can cut these using a special compressor without radically altering the song's soundscape.

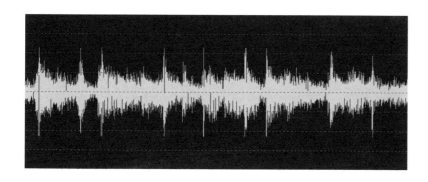

Peaks are ironed out and the master signal can be boosted.

Then you can hike the overall level so the compressed peaks level off at the odB threshold. This increases the average level of the song significantly.

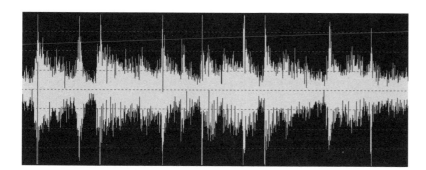

◎ CD
Track 16: Original recording
Track 17: Level boosted by
6dB using a compressor.
Track 18: Level boosted by
12dB; slight distortion is
audible.

Mastering compressors like Wave's "L1 Ultramaximizer" and "Peak Master" in Wavelab let you cut off peaks and bring the volume up to the maximum level in one go. The result can be written directly into a new file.

All that remains to be done is to dump the processed files to your master medium. This couldn't be any easier if you own a computer with a CD burner and your mastering program offers the option of burning CDs.

FAQ

5

What are the advantages of digital recording?

Even if according to conventional wisdom analog recordings sound warmer, digital recording has many advantages in the home studio: No tape hiss, no sound degradation through wear and tear of the recording medium, and loss-free tracking.

My digital recording device gives me a choice of different resolutions (16 or 24 bits) and different sampling frequencies (44.1, 48 or 96kHz). What's best for my purposes?

Audio CDs use 16 bits and 44.1kHz. If you aim for your final product to be a CD—regardless if you toast it at home or have it mass-produced in a pressing factory—16 bits and 44.1kHz should get the job done for your recordings.

The term "latency" is often mentioned in connection with computer-based recording. What's that all about?

Computers don't process audio signals in real time. It takes the CPU some time to compute functions such as effects and EQ'ing. That delay in the time it takes to generate a processed signal is called latency. Depending on hardware and software architecture, latency can range from a few milliseconds and to several tenths of a second.

Whenever I record vocals or acoustic guitars with a microphone, I hear soft music in the background of the recorded track. How can I avoid this?

The problem is that the sound from the headphones is spilling into the microphone. The solution is to use closed headphones with big shells that seal as tightly as possible around the ears. You can also turn headphones signal as low as the given musician finds acceptable.

When I change the position of an aux send knob on the mixer, this affects not only the intensity of the assigned effect but also the volume of the instrument on this track. Why is that?

When you're using effects plugged into an aux bus, you must turn the original signal (dry) all the way down on the processor via the dry/wet knob. This way you can be sure that only the wet signal is being sent back via the aux return.

Why do professional recordings always sound louder and punchier than my tracks even though I mix them at maximum level (0dB)?

Professional audio engineers use special compressors to cut signal peaks, which allows them to boost the overall volume of the song considerably.

Internet Links

6

Home Recording and Related Issues

http://recordingwebsite.com/index.html   Many home and studio recording articles and links, chat room

http://www.homerecording.com/   Lots of articles and links on the subject of home recording

http://www.audioamigo.com/   Discussion forum, lots of links

http://www.sweetwater.com/support/techlib/   Articles and links

Effects

http://www.recordingwebsite.com/articles/eqprimer.html   All about equalizers and their many uses

http://arts.ucsc.edu/ems/music/equipment/signal_processors/processors_intro/processors.html   The lowdown on equalizers and dynamics effects

http://www.digido.com/compression.html   Articles on employing compressors while mastering

Microphones

http://www.sweetwater.com/support/techlib/ Tips on miking pianos, acoustic guitars, and vocals

http://arts.ucsc.edu/EMS/Music/tech_background/TE-20/teces_20.html Technical tips on microphones

Free Plug-ins

http://www.mda-vst.com/ VST plug-ins

http://www.netcologne.de/~nc-rehaagth/tr.htm VST plug ins

http://www.espace-cubase.org/freesuppos.php3 French site, VST plug-ins

Basic Knowledge

http://recordingeq.com/glossary/glosae.htm Glossary

http://www.digido.com/cdmastering.html Mastering

http://www.recordingwebsite.com/articles/shapemix.html Tips on mixing vocals

http://www.sweetwater.com/publications/Technical%20Information/articles/recording_guide.html#cables Recording Guide by Roger Nichols; many useful tips and tricks